Prozac Poetry

Kenzie Mac.

hello.

This book is dedicated to the lovers of poetry, the black
sheep, the outcasts, and those who just
Need to feel a little less alone.

Grab a blanket and a cup of Earl Grey and come along
for the ride.

The Poems.

If i could
Id slide into your skin
And think of myself

See how your body reacts
see if it tears you up inside thinking of me
see if your intestines knot and loop

if your cheeks get hot and your brain curdles
If your tongue dries and shrivels
And acid burns the back of your throat

If it makes you sick to think
Of the things you said to me
If it makes your chest tight

If the thought of me feels
Like a thousand knives
In your stomach

I want to know
If you regret it

Or if you even think
Of me at all.

She makes you feel like that time
You stood in an art gallery, alone
For hours, breathless,
speechless, stunned at the
Wonders around you.

Serpentine structure
Carved by the gods
Chiselled away so painstakingly
Each tap motivated
By the desire to create
Something more beautiful than words
Could ever demonstrate.

So silken, when fingers brushed,
It was hard to tell whether she was really
Touching your skin
Or whether you were
Caressing the air.

Each flaw hand painted with such loving precision
Thin silver lightning bolts down her hip
Where she grew to make way for new life

Pale pink scar, where she chipped herself
As a child, climbing trees with her brother.

Not a single mark on her was accidental
All were placed with beautiful purpose.

Monochrome girl
Gives nothing away.

She laughs when she's supposed to
Bats her eyes when she's supposed to
Keeps herself coated
In a thick layer
Of pink
Like she's supposed to

Blends in perfectly
With every shade
From blush to magenta
Just like she's supposed to.

Only talks about boys
Like she's supposed to

Monochrome girl
Dyes her hair peach
paints her nails Ruby
Slips on a bubblegum
Dress
And tucks a carnation behind
Her ear

Trying not to acknowledge
The kaleidoscope of
Colour her skin
Had become.
Just like she's supposed to.

I am tangled up with you.

As tangled as our nose rings were that night in the back of
your car and all we could do was laugh and kiss and laugh.

As tangled as our limbs, in comfort,
intertwined soft loops of headphones in your pocket.

As tangled as our paths that led us here paved with
heartache.

As tangled as our string, making braids of our futures,
interlacing us together.

Draught under door makes
Candle flames dance

Sound of rain against the glass

Rise and fall of gentle chest

Intertwined, our time to rest.

That first sip of hot sweet tea

Bones sink into cushion seats

Some unlit fire crackles low

Our movement tender, soft and slow.

Your breath as tranquil as the sea

The truth is, you are home to me.

Notice her.

Bronzer chiselling cheekbones, pout lined and plumped
with a shade of pink/red/beige you can't quite put your
finger on

Stars in her eyes and on her earrings as stories pour out of
her mouth and she laughs and makes you feel like there's
nowhere else you'd rather be in the world than by her side,
Just noticing her.
Really noticing her.

the poorly concealed under eye purple
Blooming lilac from
Dreams that hurt more than a fist ever could.

The laugh so loud to drown out the way
Her brain is telling her
she doesn't really belong here.

The still red and raised welts
On arms and thighs
That clearly show she's still trying so hard to heal and the
smoke on her breath that whispers she's finding other ways
to hurt herself from the inside out anyway while the stars in
her eyes start to flicker and burn out like candles being
suffocated

Because she knows you noticed and it's so hard to disguise
the fear of being left for just being you.

Subtle tingle
Lingers
Where your lips
Pressed against mine
I can still taste you
Long after you drive
Away
Some unknown
Emptiness
Takes over
A longing
As though my bones
Are tied to yours
String stretched
Taut.
This unexplainable pull
Unravelling the pathways
Of my body
Like the yarn on my old favourite jumper
Snagging on twigs
Of reality
Sharp splinters
Of proof that
This is more damaging
Than love should be
But my fumbling fingers
Still desperately try to braid us back together
As though
This could ever fall back into place.

Every landing perfectly planned
Each drop a kiss projected
from the heavens
Determined aim

Hailstorm beauty

Deftly dances atop the leaves
Sunkissed hues of green
Glow with ethereal beauty
As she gracefully descends
With powerful purpose

Falls to the floor
Her dance ending
As she gives herself
To the Earth

Ready to begin again.

Forlorn petal
Dried and cracked from baking sun
Desert dry
Too much of a good thing.

Wilted under weight of hot air
Struggle to breathe
Spoiled by Helios
His kiss bleaching
Colours away

Atmosphere sticking
On your skin
Like honey.

Sky lights up purple
A deafening roar
In the distance
As first drop

Lands perfectly
On sun shaped centre

Quenching thirst
You never knew existed.

A gift
From Zeus.

There's a certain pressure
Urging at the forefront of
My skull
Pressing against the bone
Begging to be released
Tip of the tongue
Partial recall

Desperate to take shape
To be said out loud
Become real

Dancing along the
Razor edge of my teeth

Mind grows hands
Moulding thoughts
Like clay
That keeps collapsing
Inward

It's not that I don't want to
Talk about it

It's that I don't know how

Almost find the words
Feel them graze
Against my lips

Then slips out
of my insubstantial grasp.

I ran away today.
Collected all of the loose change i had to my name
Used it to fuel my car
And just drove.

Stumbled upon
A forest
Where I traipsed through the undergrowth
Cutting ankles on thorns
Lost
In both body and mind

But happy.

Walking down paths
In my memory
That felt as brand new
As the unfamiliar
Ground beneath me

Still comforted
That the earth
Is where we all return to
Anyway
So it doesn't really matter
If you don't know where you're going

Because not many of us do.

The day my brain cracked
I awoke to the sounds of
My children's laughter
And ignored it
Waiting for him
To tend to them.

Their happiness felt
Like too much.

I laid and watched
As my opened window
Allowed the rain to
Take up residency
In my carpet
And wished it was me
That was dripping
Underneath
The floorboards.

I saw his face
As he popped his head
Round the door frame
To make sure I was still
Breathing
And found me
In the same position
As hours before
Still alive

on the outside.

The day my brain cracked
Guilt was the driving motivation
As I pulled myself up
Out of depressions soft
Warm grip
And nourished my body
With the happiness
That resided one
Floor below me

It still felt like too much
Differently this time

More than I deserved

Pure, unbreakable,
Trusting love
That pulled me back
From the brink.

We tuck ourselves under covers
Building dens like children
Block out the feelings
Scream into the duvet
Knowing you've soundproofed
This fort with so many pillows
Nobody will hear it anyway

Scream until there's nothing left
Scream until it's funny
Til laughter is the thing
Hurting your throat
It's so goddamn funny
Because you're the
One who put so much effort

Perfecting this spot
Where nobody can reach you
When all you want is
Someone to push through
Lost yourself there

Deserted island
You and your blanket
Washed out to sea
Quilt so used
To soaking up tears
It's become waterproof
Anyway

Waiting
For what exactly, you don't know.

Freeze.
It's my go to
Incapable of making a decision
Words caught in my throat
Like a fish in a net
Trapped
Thrashing, panic
Pathetic,desperate attempts
at escape

Sandpaper tongue
Dries up any attempt
At speech
Feel my body wilt
Like a wallflower

My poker face so perfected
You'd never know their
Were wolves inside the
Walls of my stomach
Snarling and snapping
Over who will
Take charge

Only sign of my fear
The twitch of my pulse
As my heart hammers.

I find myself
At 10:52
Composing messages that
I know I won't send

Thoughts like meteors
Raining down
Colliding with my brain and landing
With a sick, solid punch
To the gut

Feel my skin blister
As the fire spreads
Red hot glow begins to
Encase the world
Around us

I thought that your life was supposed to flash
Before your eyes but the only thing
Flashing is my anger
Mimicking the heat
I'm surrounded by

Feel my pulse raise
Sweat drip and puddle
Lava rise in my throat
Feel it scald its way out

Scorches open Pandora's box

Let's every molecule of my energy
Combust and explode

Second guessing my own pain
Playing the main role
In my own extinction

Perfect personality
Carved up by the tragedy
Became, I guess, a martyr
There's comfort in "alone"

Apparent abnormality
Black sheep of the family
Hurting yourself don't matter
If it isn't to the bone

Faulty functionality
lost myself to apathy
somewhere between the river
and the road to home

Slip and sliding sanity
Caught up in the fantasy
I cast a prayer upstream
Watched the water foam

Pathetic in my fallacy
Betrayed by my anatomy
Too cowardly to journey
Instead, I carry on.

I found a rock in my garden
And I know it's just a rock
But something about it makes me
Feel as though it was delivered by
The hands of God herself
Dropped in dewy grass
For me to find

And despite everything I know
Or don't know, I suppose,
There's something so enticing
Confusing,
Heavenly,
In it's black sparkle
Like a little piece of
Magic
Fallen through black holes
To make it's way
Through the skies
And down to
My feet.

It's 4am
And your hands are on my waist
Fingertips light
My skin like memory foam
Where you belong

Until your hands turn into his
And this memory foam skin
Remembers too much

Your fingers, though gentle
Start to burn
My spongy soft flesh
Until nothing is left
But ash

And those god damn memories

"No trespassing"
Regardless of the sign
brambles around my ankles
I carry on
Keep walking
Right now this is where I need to be
Right here
In this moment
Barefoot
Blindfolded
Feel the soft mud against my skin, grounded
Navigate by intuition
Mother Earth whispers
The way in my ear
Confident in my step
Soak in the golden sun
Peace in a clearing
Where I lay my sins out
And watch them
Drip down my cheeks
Ready to fertilise new life
In the soil.

Contorted, bound
Rope on flesh
Grazed and burned
Masochistic magic
Anticipation
Left on the edge
A mess
A blur
All hands on wrists
Grasping tight
Teeth sink into flesh
Aching, twitching
Agony, arousal
Hunger for more
"Tighter"

Leave me breathless

She greets me
Silvery glow received by my skin
Poured like honey, iridescent
Drips and dances its way down

Something magnificent in the way
She waxes, wanes,
Changing face as she pleases
All of them bewitching

She comforts me
Crisp biting chill of the dark
As she listens to my sins
And why I'm friends with 2am

And before she leaves
She holds me in her light
Her push/pull of the rolling waves
Lull my heavy eyes once more.

We compared ourselves to supernovas

Galaxies in our eyes

Making constellations of our flaws

Said our hearts were like black holes

All-consuming and unexplainable

Burning, collapsing into ourselves

Never once taking a moment to realise

How beautiful we made the sky look.

//Hands//
Rough, calloused, dirt lodged under snapped nails
Digging my way out of the hole I woke in
Born again, kick the wood
Persistent, climbing
Ignore the sting
Rocks slice palms
Accidental,

On

//Wrists//
Not quite as mistaken
Bubbling hot fury
Misdirected at myself
Belts of desperation
Laced across my skin
Soldiers lined for battle
Running drills fight or flight
Heart beat, drum of war
Set up camp, rest and grow

//Teeth//
Begin to cut
Keeps me from sleep
Who knew a third set existed
Reaching higher planes
Of existence
Gums leak crimson
Metallic taste
Growth worth every ounce of pain.

He appears on the doorstep
Uninvited as always
And lets himself in through an open window

Kicks his shoes off at the door leaving them where they lay
and makes himself a home in your bed

A heavy weight,
dip in your mattress,
rolling towards him in your sleep, keeping you awake with
his constant stream of mumbles under his breath making
you feel restless
And you refuse to acknowledge his presence, this cannot be
real
Perfect denial until

You see dirty dishes he's strewn across the worktop, feel your
skin blister from the boiling of your blood scorching its way
through your body fighting its way to the surface
pressure building volcano begging to erupt as you shatter
every dish with a strength you never knew you had
"Why the fuck wasn't it me?"

feel the echo of an empty home scream back at you

And grief watches from the corner, smug.
takes your hand, stops you from trying to clean, pulls you
back in to that bed and holds you so tight it almost starts to
feel like comfort, whispers sadness in your ear,

And stays as long as he pleases,

Before departing
with a piece of you in his pocket

And a promise
"I'll be back before you know it"

I guess I just feel as though I'm watering dead roots

with my sweat and my blood and my tears and my hope
Pouring buckets of myself out, filling them back up,
Praying for a shoot

And all I'm getting back is brittle twigs, dry and bare and
snapping in the breeze, soil like quick sand absorbing my
soul, sucking in all life, thriving off my energy, making
fertiliser of my flesh tearing myself apart trying to make this
grow

but it's still not enough to make this tree

bear fruit.

Feeling warm light
reflect, refract,
Sending prisms of light glancing over your face
Eyes closed, breath slow

Pulse twitching, lets you know you're alive

Soak it in,
focus on how your brain feels like static,
how your body feels like static,
How your thoughts are like static,
Running through your wire veins sparks igniting praying
you don't combust but knowing you wouldn't really mind if
you did

Electric charge
Lying in wait at the tips of your fingers
Blue lightning arcs and twitches
Over your palms

Begging for someone to take that one step too close.

pink
like your brain
that keeps urging, insisting
It is not alone
That someone is with you
Crawling through the maze above your head
Bed
Quick
Replace it
With another thought, desperately trying, what can I taste
what can I feel
Pink
Like your tongue
That asked him to search
For the monster hiding in your wardrobe, sleeping under
your bed, folded up in the cupboard with the towels waiting
until you're alone to pounce from the shadows
Quick
Pink
Like your heart
How it swelled when he salted and lined the doors of every
single one of those places just to make sure you felt safe even
though he knew the only thing you really feared was
Pink
Like your brain.

And I still dream about him
Panic running through me
Blood turned to jelly
Wobbly, weak
The way snake venom reacts

Sweat seeps out of pores
Waking alone, panting and sweating

His screaming voice
His anger parasitic
Frozen in fear
He feeds off it
Like a T-bone steak

Raw and bloodied
Dripping down his face
Tasting the terror
And I can see it satisfy him

Until the next time.

It's funny what you remember.

Not what we argued over,
But the colour of my dress (burgundy)
And that the weather was pathetic fallacy
at its finest.

Not the reason I walked out of the house,
But my intended last text (I love you, I'm sorry)
And slipping off my coat and shoes,
Perched on the dirty river bank.

Not taking a step toward the nearly-bursting river,
But your voice (what the fuck are you doing?)
And how I crumbled into you as the sky wept
You ran back for my shoes.

Not deciding to walk there again today,
But stepping on the edge (careful, don't slip)
And thinking that
The view from up here will not be my last.

Oh God I crave you.

Fingertips like fire,
brushing, burning
into my paper skin
leaving behind singed corners,
trailing ash,
pain and pleasure.

Frenzied, hot breath,
No time to stop for air.

I feel myself fall into you.
Your touch,
your tongue,
your teeth,
Grazing my bottom lip.

I douse myself in petrol.
I light the match.

We burn together.

To those I love
I am an ear,
An embrace,
A shoulder,
The warmth of a cup of hot tea
Pressed against your hand.

I am still waiting for the day
That those I love
Love me enough to see.

See that I am Van Gogh,
Poised with razor to my listening ear.

That my embrace is laced with desperation.

That my shoulder you weep into
Is already soaked
From the floods of my own heartbreak.

See that as you drink your tea,
My cup is filled with yellow paint,
Praying to wash away the sadness.

Is anyone listening?

A skull, decayed and broken
Laying on the dirty ground,
Filthy and forgotten.

Hollow, stripped of its flesh,
Ravaged by nature,
Left with nothing more to offer.

Untouched so long,
That out of the empty vessel,
New life began to bloom.

Fertilised by the loss,
Sheltered by the empty cavern,
Beauty took up its root.

Filling every dark space with vibrant colour
Reaching from the ground toward the light.

Up, from the ashes.

Sweet 16 and dewy-eyed
Desperation to belong
Uprooted and re-planted
In a smaller pot than I began in.

Surrounded by hills bigger than
I'd ever even seen
Vast open spaces for miles
Dropped in a town of 2,000

The stars in that tiny place
Would take your breath away
Leave you reeling at the infinity
Of the midnight blue

The people and the places
The faces and the names
Are etched into my bones
Beautiful memories I hold so dear

The moon is the same moon
Wherever you go.

But the crushing weight
Of city life
Makes me desperately
Crave home.

It wasn't where I was born but goddamn, it's where I was
raised.

Killjoy is what he calls me
after I cocked my head sweetly to the side and asked "why is
that funny?"
And I silently
add killjoy to the list of names I've been called, under
Loud Brash Bossy Bitchy
And my personal favourite, dramatic
When I stood in a restaurant kitchen at 16
And screamed at the owner
For wrapping his hands around my waist
And pressing against me as I washed dishes in the sink
And he tried to tell me I was making it up
That he was just squeezing past me
Squeezing past me so tight I could smell the liquor on his
breath?
I don't think so
And if screaming that he is not entitled to my personal space
makes me dramatic then give me a crown because I'm the
fucking queen.
Hysterical
Hormonal
Must be her time of the month
How dare you shrink my anger
Make it seem worthless
Irrelevant
A product of an unsound mind
Tell me again how you'd obliterate the man who dares to
speak to your daughter that way
Now tell me why you need to be reminded that I am
somebody's daughter, somebody's partner, before you
remember that I'm a person

If demanding the respect I'm entitled to in a room full of
men who are given it freely makes me a killjoy then I'll wear
that title like a badge of honour.

lost eyes graze across carpet obscured by unpaid bills, each
breath leaving tendrils in the icy, inky dark of his house
and it almost feels like a metaphor but this is his reality,
hope so lost he cannot even find a reason to keep the lights
on.

You've been detained under section 2 of the mental health
act okay, my love? Do you remember what that means from
before?

"There's nothing anyone can do for me any more"
Lost eyes suddenly focus and it's clear this is the one thing
he believes is true

Arms looped either side by two daughters, barely adults
themselves holding up the patriarch of their family.

The eldest turns to us
"It's almost Christmas and there is food in his fridge from
September"
"Please make sure he eats"
But no tears wet their cheeks, it's clear this is a dance they
have done before
As they help him into the van, "please try to get better dad"
And as she kisses him goodbye she slips a chocolate bar in his
pocket, hope on her face.

And as the door closes and we roll away, he notices, and for
the first time smiles

"my favourite"
and takes a bite.

Acknowledgments

Cover image Hand bottle photo created by nakaridore - www.freepik.com.

www.ingramcontent.com/pod-product-compliance
Lightning Source LLC
Chambersburg PA
CBHW031516150726
47990CB00007B/3041